T0128473

THE FLU VACCINE CHANGED MY LIFE

A Retired Military Spouse's Story of How the Flu Shot Changed Her Life and the Life of Her 20 Year Veteran Husband

Donna White McGinnis

WESTBOW
P R E S S®
A DIVISION OF THOMAS NELSON
& ZONDERVAN

Scriptures taken from the Holy Bible, New International Version®, NIV®.
Copyright © 1973, 1978, 1984, 2011 by Biblica, Inc.™ Used by permission
of Zondervan. All rights reserved worldwide. www.zondervan.com
The "NIV" and "New International Version" are trademarks registered
in the United States Patent and Trademark Office by Biblica, Inc.™

WestBow Press books may be ordered through booksellers or by contacting:

WestBow Press
A Division of Thomas Nelson & Zondervan
1663 Liberty Drive
Bloomington, IN 47403
www.westbowpress.com
1 (866) 928-1240

ISBN: 978-1-9736-4609-9 (sc)
ISBN: 978-1-9736-4608-2 (e)

Print information available on the last page.

WestBow Press rev. date: 11/19/2018

Giving true honor to God, who is the head of my life. I thank you God for holding my hand, walking with me, and for the days that I was just so weak and felt like I couldn't go on, you picked me up in your arms and carried me. Thank you my Heavenly Father!

DEDICATION

I would like to dedicate this book to the love of my life, Melvin McGinnis, Sr. for his courage to keep fighting and not giving up on life no matter how bad his illness was and still is despite his daily suffering. Melvin, you are a true man of God, a man of faith, a loving husband, and a wonderful father to our two children, Melvin Jr. and Shermiah. I salute and thank you for your 20 years of service in the UNITED STATES ARMY. You served your country faithfully and with pride and I will always be forever proud and I will always love you, my darling.

Donna

CONTENTS

INTRODUCTION

This book is based on the life and health of my husband Melvin, a retired Army Soldier and the struggle he has been facing after receiving a Flu Vaccine, and the hard time I have endured during my husband's illness.

Five years ago, my husband became physically ill after receiving a shot. If someone would have told me that our world was going to come tumbling down, I would have said that's not true. And then it happened, everything started to fall apart, I just could not believe what was before my eyes, this bad vaccine took over my husband's life and my life, and because he was so sick, I took on the responsibility of being my husband's caregiver. I had no idea my job would be so difficult and painful. I started to feel as if we were being punished, but in my heart I know that is not true because we are not given more than we can bear. But later I had to learn how to be a nurse overnight in order to take care of my husband, and because I love him so dearly, I had no problem taking on this task.

Sometimes being a caregiver, there are things that you would say to yourself like: I would not be able to do this, this is too hard, or I can't do this because my stomach won't let me. But take it from a person who has said all those things, and when it comes to caring for the people you love that thought will quickly leave your mind.

There are times when my husband had to be admitted to the hospital, I had to be away from our daughter and that was hard, but I felt I had no choice because my husband was giving up on life, and I wanted to give him hope so he would not leave my children and me.

TO MY ONE AND ONLY TRUE LOVE

Loving you Melvin
Loving you Melvin is everything to me. Loving you Melvin brings me so much joy even when you are not at your best.

Loving you Melvin for 30+ years has a connection with no end because the love we have is so deep and true.

Loving you Melvin for the person you are makes me thank God every day for blessing me and putting you in my life.

Loving you Melvin is a joy, you always supported me in all of my dreams making them all a reality

Loving you Melvin makes me proud to be your wife and mother of our beautiful children

Loving you Melvin has always kept a smile on my face, you never said an unkind word, you never complained, and you were always my motivator, my soul mate forever

Loving you Melvin is forever and ever.

Our wedding day, July 21, 1984

My uncle Willie (my father's brother) performed the
wedding ceremony. He passed away in 1995.

CHAPTER 1
TAKING THE OATH

Melvin grew up in a small town in Alabama, Frisco City. Melvin was very quiet and observant. He was very smart and enjoyed learning. Melvin grew up with four brothers and one sister. He was the second child of six. He and his family loved to go fishing and hunting. During high school, Melvin enjoyed playing football and after graduation in 1976, Melvin was unable to attend college because he could not afford it, so after getting permission from his parents at the age of 16, Melvin enlisted in the United States Army and made a career out of it.

Enlisting in the United States Army at the age of 16 was not unusual, during that time a lot of graduating seniors could not afford to further their education so most of them joined the armed forces. By 1983, Melvin decided that he wanted a break from the army, so in 1983 he was granted a honorable discharge, he then moved back to his home Frisco city, Alabama. He joined the Army National Guard and worked at a local factory.

CHAPTER 2
LOVE AT FIRST SIGHT

My memorable moment about Melvin is back in 1980. I was out on a date at the club sitting at the table, and while looking across the room there were four young men walking, but only one stood out. Oh he was so handsome I could not take my eyes off him then it was like he vanished into thin air never to see him anymore. Then three years later this good looking man appeared again at his brother's wedding reception. We danced and fell deeply in love. It was love at first sight, we had been watching each other all during the night. Melvin was the DJ and later this handsome young man walked up and asked, may I have this dance while this beautiful slow song was playing I said yes, he pull me close to him, he was so strong and smelled so good, I was smiling, not knowing that he would one day be my husband. On July 21, 1984, wedding bells were ringing, Melvin married me (Donna), his sweetheart of Atmore, Alabama, and 33 years later we are still in love and loving each other.

CHAPTER 3
SECOND TIME AROUND

In 1985, Melvin reenlisted active duty in the United States Army before leaving for Korea. Melvin had already served so he knew what to expect, so it came easy for him to get back into the flow of things. Melvin was proud to serve his country, and he knew that while serving his country he could provide a better life for his family. This would be a new adventure for me, not only were we newly married, but now I am a military spouse.

Our very first duty station was Fort Lewis, Washington. We drove across country which was exciting and sad. It was my first time being away from my parents and it was such a long long way. It was a big difference from my hometown, Atmore, AL. I had to get used to being alone because my husband being a combat engineer was away most of the time. I had to learn and become familiar with Fort Lewis on my own. The people were nice; we lived in housing, and despite the horror stories that you hear about housing, we got ours pretty fast because I was six months pregnant. I had to get used to the rainy days, it must have rained every day. The rainy days made me more homesick. I was so glad to see my husband when he came through the doors from work. He would just light up the room and brighten my day. When it snowed it was a lot of it, but I must say nothing compared to Alaska. In September 1986, while stationed there, I gave birth to our first child, a handsome baby boy. I also found employment, which made the time go by.

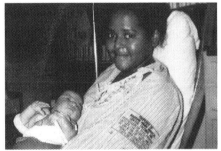

Daddy's boy, Lil' Melvin was born (what's so funny?)

CHAPTER 4
"SMOOTH" DRILL SERGEANT

In 1990, Melvin became a Drill Sergeant and he was transferred to Fort Leonard Wood, Missouri. Oh my goodness, it was really Fort Lost in the Woods, the nickname it had been given. The only thing there was a clothing store, grocery store, car dealerships, clubs, and loan places.

I went to school and got my cosmetologist license and worked as a hair stylist while we were stationed there. Being the wife of a drill sergeant was not always easy, the nights were long and cold without him, but because of his love for training the basic trainees I understood. I enjoyed the cycle breaks because that meant that we would be able to go out and spend quality time with Melvin, Jr., who just adored his dad. He enjoyed putting on the round-brown, his dad's drill sergeant hat. He also went to work and mocked his dad when he would tell the trainees to drop down and give me 20 push-ups. They all enjoyed it and there was much laughter when my husband's fellow drill sergeants and the trainees would hear this little boy giving orders.

As I said earlier, the cycle breaks were great because my husband was also able to enjoy his hobbies, especially fishing. He would clean the fish and it was great when he cooked them, and he also made his mouth-watering, great tasting hushpuppies. It would be so nice if I could just taste one of those hushpuppies again, and most of all see him smiling and cooking fish the way he used to, I do believe in miracles and I am not giving up.

Scripture- John 14:12-24- Verily, verily, I say unto you, He that believeth on me, the works that I do shall he do also; and greater [works] than these shall he do; because I go unto my Father.

My husband enjoying being a drill sergeant. It was one of the highlights of his career.

CHAPTER 5
MR. DEEP-SEA FISHERMAN

In 1993, after Melvin took off the round brown, his drill sergeant hat, we PCSed further away, to Fort Richardson, Alaska. We would be there for three years. We had to get used to Alaska, especially the snow. It was always a lot to do, nothing like it was in Missouri. Melvin really enjoyed it. He became a deep-sea fisherman over there. He caught so many fish, really huge fish.

Oh so many fish, fish to clean, cook and to
eat! He had a great fishing day!

"Help, I'm seasick", my husband was sick for three days!

He was very glad to return back and to see this sign

Exciting things were going on in Alaska, the Iditarod Trail Sled
Dog Race.
My husband also reenlisted there.

I owned my own business there, so it was a great time. Life was great! I wish for those great times now. It is so hard seeing my husband not enjoying life the way he used to, the way we used to. Will he ever be able to go to a concert or to a comedy show again? We did so much traveling, he saw the Iditarod (Alaska Dog Sled Racing) over there. Unfortunately, I missed out, I was at work. Melvin Jr. loved Alaska; he did not want to leave. He enjoyed playing with his dad and friends out in the snow. There are so many memorable events that we experienced there, and I try to hold on to those memories every day, but when I go into my bedroom, and I look into his eyes, as I touch his tender hand, and hear his soft voice, reality is there. I pray this, I look to you God, and I say the scripture at the bottom of the page. I have to hold on to it.

Philippians 4:13
I can do all things through Christ who strengthens me.

Lil' Melvin enjoyed playing in the snow in Alaska

Daddy's boy, enjoying the moment that daddy caught and brought home a big salmon!

Catch of the day, Ship Creek (in Alaska)

Melvin at the Alaska Pipeline

CHAPTER 6
A NEW BEGINNING IS NEAR

After leaving Fort Richardson, Alaska with my bundle of joy rolling around inside of me and arriving to Fort Benning, GA, I gave birth to a beautiful, bouncy, and bubbly baby girl, Shermiah. Shermiah is a daddy's girl. Her dad was and still is her biggest cheerleader. His face lights up at the mention of her name. She is her dad's twin. She looks like him, has height like him, smiles like him, and has so many of his ways, maybe I should have named her Melvina, oh my I wonder would she have liked it, I know he would have. Shermiah, like her dad and brother is very athletic, playing softball and volleyball. Melvin was able to make it to the very last game before her graduation, he was determined to see her even if it was not from the stands but sitting along the side in his wheelchair. All through her high school years, he was very ill, we did not know if he was going to make it. I could tell that it was very painful for him not to enjoy his baby girl's high school years the way he really wanted to. It was painful for all of us to watch him miss out on what should have been one of the happiest times of his life. Shermiah used to cry, she thought that he was going to die. It was so painful for her after always seeing this tall, strong, and very energetic daddy, to see him feeble, weak, and disoriented, a man that she knew as her father, but nothing like the man that she grew up seeing, hearing his laughter, and most of all holding her in his arms. I am thankful that my husband did not give up and he continued to hold on to his faith. Times like these can make a person just give up the fight, but he, we held on, we held on to each other and most of all our faith.

Hebrews 11:1-Now faith is the substance of things hoped for, the evidence of things not seen.

Daddy's baby girl!
Lil Melvin is now a big brother; see how happy he is.......

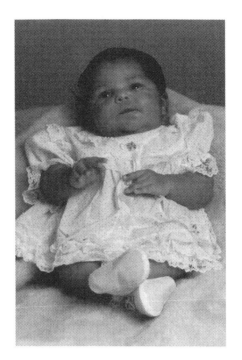

Baby girl experiencing mom's skills

Daddy's girl is
growing up

Shermiah and her dad
back at their favorite
spot; it was a tradition
to take a picture each
year at the same place.

Shermiah is just like her dad and brother very athletic

CHAPTER 7
RETIREMENT DAY HAS COME

In July 1998, Melvin retired at Fort Benning, Georgia as a Sergeant First Class, from the United States Army after serving 20 years. Retirement, what should have been the greatest time of our lives, was the most painful. Standing on the stage at McGinnis-Wickham Hall, all of us, proud of my husband, proud of my children's father, looking forward to working in my profession, life after the military, thanking the one above in the heavens for the great times and memories that we would share, What seemed to be the perfect day, seeing him smiling, shaking hands with friends, co-workers, fellow soldiers; never in a million years I would have or even could have imagined that my husband would be the very sick man that he is today.

Receiving my diploma for Advanced Cosmetology Training
from Mr. Joe Dudley, founder of Dudley University

CHAPTER 8
A PRICE TO PAY

After retirement, Melvin continued working at a local bakery so he could provide for his family. On October 25, 2011, while at his place of work the company was offering the flu vaccine. So, before coming home, Melvin decided to take a flu shot the same as he always did for the last twenty years in the military, because he wanted to stay healthy and being a loyal employee to his employer he didn't want to catch the flu and cause his coworkers to become sick and spread the germs into the products in the bakery.

Even now, when I look at this pink piece of paperwork, I can only think of how it changed our lives forever; when we hear of pink slips we think of someone losing their jobs but when I hear pink slip I think about how my husband has suffered and is still suffering.

When Melvin returned home from work, he was complaining of having this excruciating headache and not feeling well. The next morning, his throat had become very sore and scratchy. He began to cough badly and a few days later the high fevers and shortness of breath had started. Melvin and I thought maybe it was just a cold after taking the flu shot because those symptoms and reactions were common is what we always heard and that it would soon go away but something happened. This would change our lives forever.

Melvin's joints and hands started to swell until he was

unable to lift or pick up anything because of the pain that was so excruciating.

Within two weeks, Melvin's condition was getting worse so I took him to see his doctor. Despite everything Melvin was going through, he continued trying to work, although his body was weak and he was in pain, he was determined to support his family. Soon, it became very difficult for Melvin to do his job so his coworker would pitch in and help him so he could get a paycheck. Melvin worked until he just could not go anymore.

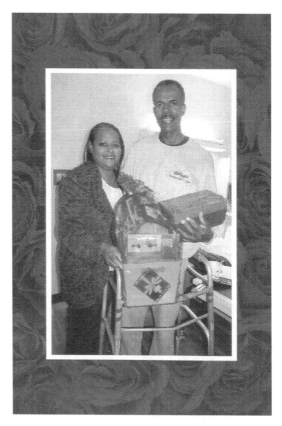

Melvin's co-worker's kindness and support will never be forgotten. Words can never express our gratitude.

Melvin had made so many trips to the emergency room and to see his doctor that it was routine for the family. By November 2011, Melvin's health was declining, even more so he had to stop work, which led to financial hardship, because his job was the only source of income. It had become very hard for Melvin to get out of bed and walk without my help. Many thoughts ran across my mind, I was confused, depressed, and just wished that I could just wake up, this has to be a dream. I could only cry out for strength. While driving to the hospital, I had feelings of great sadness knowing that my husband would soon be lying in a hospital fighting for his life, and that was sad because my heart was hurting for him, and to this day, my heart is still hurting just as much as before seeing Melvin in a vulnerable state of mind, and watching my husband struggle with a mysterious illness is very confusing and frustrating. This is something a person could not ever imagine happening to them. I know it is not fair as to what happened to Melvin, but I can be strong for him while I am in his presence, also as sick as my husband was, a part of me thought to myself that this is it and what will my children and I do without him because his illness was very critical. I remember driving back home from a hospital in Birmingham to prepare our children for the news of their daddy's condition and the days ahead, and all I could do was cry, because I didn't know how I was going to tell Melvin and Shermiah that their father might not make it. That was one of the most difficult things I ever had to do. But once more my faith sustained and brought me through.

Melvin had other problems that had started to occur. He was losing weight at a rapid pace.

He was so sick that he could not eat. Later Melvin got where he just could not remember simple things like his name, phone number, and address. I just could not understand how such a healthy 53 year old man could get so sick after getting a flu vaccine. Not only was he very ill, but he didn't look like a man in his 50s, he looked like a man in his late seventies or early eighties. On December 17, 2011, Melvin's health was getting worse day by day. He was admitted to the hospital in Georgia because of how sick he had gotten during his hospital stay. Melvin was given a bone test because the doctor thought Melvin had some form of cancer and the test came back negative. I gave Praise, Praise all Praises.

CHAPTER 9
I WANT DONNA!

A few days later, Melvin was given an MRI and a cat scan because he had developed white lesions on his brain and spine.

Melvin was still very sick and the doctor couldn't explain this illness, so the doctors quarantined Melvin for a few days because they thought he was contagious, but that was not the case. Melvin was discharged and sent home, but still a very sick man. Melvin continued seeing his doctors and going to the emergency room.

On January 18, 2012, Melvin's fever had gotten extremely high during his doctor's visit, also he was very thin. The doctor told me to take Melvin to the emergency room to be admitted in the hospital for the second time.

Melvin had started to lose pigmentation on his hands and his face. Melvin's illness was becoming more severe. January 21, 2012 while in the hospital Melvin had a seizure and became unresponsive, he was unable to open his eyes. I tried my best to get my husband to open his eyes for three days, but he just could not do it, so I told Melvin how much his children and I loved him and that we need him, and still he could not open his eyes. January 24, 2012 Melvin was sent to the hospital in Atlanta, Georgia to get help. A few days later Melvin began to wake up, that was a happy day for me, but he was not the same man that I married. This was very hard for me to see my husband like this, knowing him and seeing him always strong, always smiling, happy, and joyful, this was heartbreaking, it crushed me, I felt numb, I was sad but I knew that I had to remain strong, strong for him, but I was so so hurt. It was almost like he was a child again, because I could hear my husband, my sweetheart, crying out I want Donna, I want Donna. All I could do was cry, because it was so hard to see him that way.

On February 4, 2012, Melvin was discharged and sent to the rehabilitation hospital in Columbus, Georgia, still very sick. Melvin started to make some improvement, and he was sent home to do outpatient therapy, and once more Melvin's health declined even more. May 15, 2012, I drove three hours to the Birmingham Hospital emergency room to get help for my sick husband, so he would not die and because his illness was so complex, he was admitted that night. I didn't care, I was going to get help for my husband, I was not going to sit here and watch him suffer; watch him die, oh no we are going to fight. The thing is, I was never one to drive in the city especially places like Birmingham and Atlanta but when it comes to your family and those that you love, you will do anything and put fear aside.

I just kept holding on and trusting and keeping my faith.

Hospitals became my second home. I have many experiences some good and some not so good. The hospital food was sometimes good and sometimes bad but after being at the hospital for so long I learned my way around town so that I could find better food to eat.

The people I met were very awesome because they took me a person they knew nothing about and made sure I had food to eat and money in my pocket so I could travel back home to check on our children they also would come in my husband's hospital room just to say a prayer for him.

Some of the staff were very nice to my husband and I and there were some staff members that were only there for a paycheck, they did not take care of my husband the way that he should have been taken care that is why if you have loved ones in the hospital someone needs to be with them at all times.

The smell of the hospital was sometimes overwhelmingly bad but if you have someone you love that is very sick this smell will no longer bother you because all you would think about is getting your loved one well again.

It was like a routine for Melvin and me because we stayed in the hospital almost as much as we stayed at home because every 3 to 6 months Melvin had to be admitted in the hospital due to his complex illness.

After a few days at the hospital Melvin was given a treatment called Intravenous Immunoglobulin.

CHAPTER 10

WHO TURNED OFF THE LIGHT?

On the fifth day Melvin and I were watching the T.V in his hospital room, then he asked me a strange question, he asked me where is the light? He said I can't see then his eyes became fixated so I jumped up and ran down the hall calling out for help and the medical team arrived to take care of him. This cannot be happening, not my husband losing his sight. What in the world is going on? Praises Melvin's eyesight returned the next day. About two weeks later Melvin had brain surgery, but after the surgery, he was not out of danger, the seizures started up again he was foaming at the mouth. Thoughts that were running through my head were, is my husband going to be ok? And what happened? How did we get to this point? I remember sitting in this big cold surgical waiting room wondering what's going on and asking God to please take care of my husband. I was thinking about the fact that my husband's head is being cut open, it just made chills run up and down my body. It took five hours before the doctor would come out with some news. I am thinking to myself this is the last surgery.

He was moved to ICU for several days, now I am sitting here looking at my husband on a ventilator, he was later taken off the ventilator and moved to another room.

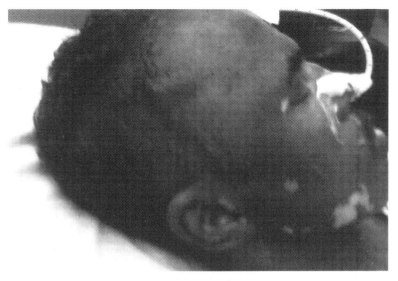

Melvin after having brain surgery

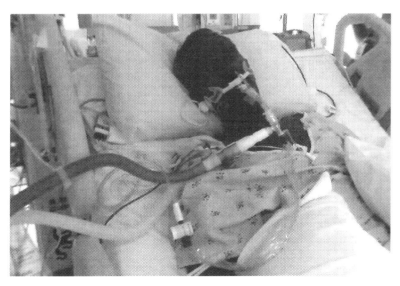

It was very hard to see my husband the strong
man that I've always known on a ventilator.

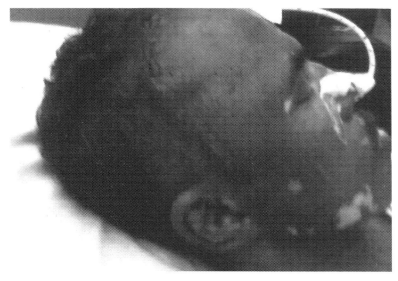

Melvin being fed through his nose.

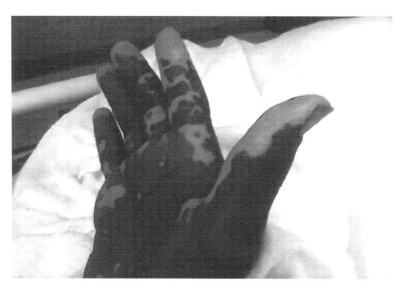

Melvin hands began to lose pigmentation

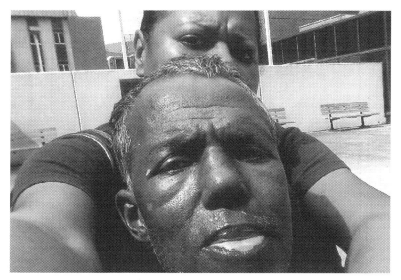

Melvin getting sunlight out on the patio at one of the hospitals that he was admitted to, he looked like he had aged 30 years.

CHAPTER 11
WHO AM I?

Melvin did not know I was his wife, to him I was his mother, his children became his brother and sister in his mind. That hurt me so bad, I had to seek help from my doctor because my husband's illness was so hard to bear. My emotional state was shattering; I was overwhelmed with pain and grief. I was becoming weak... Melvin had become bedridden and his skin had started to breakdown on his buttocks. Melvin soon developed a stage four bed sore that was very painful.

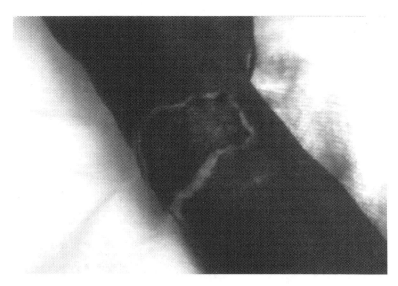

Sore on my husband's arm and other parts
of his body that later became worse.

Two weeks later Melvin's intestine perforated, and his bowels started to leak because a hole formed all the way through the stomach large bowel, and the doctor had to do emergency surgery and later he was placed on a ventilator in critical condition. I cried out, here we go again, my Melvin was back in surgery and this time it was critical, but worse than before, and had I not been there to see he was in distress, he might not have made it, because the nurse thought he was just a little agitated, but I knew he wasn't himself. I called the nurse once more and they gave Melvin a test and found out it was bad. All of this took place in 2012. Also, Melvin was given a colostomy bag and had to wear it for two years.

After Melvin recovered from surgery, the doctor gave him several biopsies on his kidneys, liver, and muscles on his forearm, and also the gland from his lip and all of tests came back negative. Melvin was still unable to walk, so by June 2012, he was moved to rehabilitation at the hospital for therapy. With little progress, Melvin was discharged to go home July 30, 2012, he was still very sick. After being home for four days, Melvin started having problems breathing, swallowing, and urinating, so I drove three hours back to the hospital in Birmingham, AL. Melvin was going into kidney, liver and respiratory failure, he was once again placed on a ventilator. I had no idea that this was happening.

Melvin's body was filled with infection, his face was swollen so big until he didn't look like the man that I had married. The next day the doctor told me this might be all they could do if the infection didn't clear up soon. I didn't want to hear that, so all I could do was cry out and look up for help. Soon, Melvin started to respond to some of the treatments the doctors gave him. Melvin was in a hospital for a total of six months before going home.

CHAPTER 12
A FAMILY'S LIFE SHATTERED

Knowing that Melvin would soon have to have another surgery was hard to accept, because Melvin and I had been married for 28 years, and he has never been sick, but little did we know that our lives would be turned upside down after taking a flu vaccine. A vaccine that is meant to prevent sickness, but this vaccine turned out to be an almost fatal ordeal for my husband, and a life changing experience for my children and me. For the last five years, I have had to do everything for my family, the support and guidance that my son and daughter would have received from their father, I had to be the one to do it. He was always there cheering them on along with me in all their school and recreational activities. They are his pride and joy, . If it hadn't been for my mom, there is no way, I could have done it, she was not only an emotional support for me, but she sacrificed her time and left her home, and came here to our home to take care of our daughter for a month, because my son was in college.

My son is an awesome young man, he sacrificed walking across the stage, and had his degree mailed to him after graduating college, so that he could come home and take care of his baby sister, and become the man of the house, filling his dad's shoes the best way he had been taught by him.

My mom, Deaconess Louise White sacrificed her time and came
and took care of Shermiah.
Thank you, mom!

I am so proud of him, I would not let him quit college, I
wanted him to finish because that was my husband and my
plans, and dream for him to get his education. We are very
proud of our daughter, she remained strong through all of
this, I wanted to make sure that she had the support that she
needed, although I knew that she longed for her daddy, but
she knew that her daddy would want her to finish school and
graduate; she graduated and now is in college. She did not like
seeing her daddy suffer, she had come to a state of mind that if
it's time and will for him to be called home to heaven, that at
least he would not be suffering any longer. It hurts me to see
her, when she stands at the door and waves to him. I know that
she may be asking the question, why did this have to happen
to my daddy? That is a question that we all have, but we still
hold on to our faith and pray that one day he will be able to
join us at the dinner table, take a family trip, and we also long
for the laughter that we all once shared.

Just when we thought things were getting better for Melvin, things gets worse. On January 24, 2013, after going to bed, Melvin started having seizures one after another. He was transported back to the hospital in Columbus, Georgia, where he was placed on a ventilator because of his respiratory failure and once again, I was so afraid for my husband's life, and because of grace, Melvin started to improve. Also, I found out to my surprise that a plate was placed in his head when he had undergone brain surgery at the hospital in Alabama. 2014 would be Melvin's last surgery, here I am again, and thinking is this really the last one? because I can't take this anymore, waiting five to six hours for the doctors to come in and give me the news.

In March 2015, just when Melvin was getting better, he got sick once again, he had gotten where he couldn't swallow water, he was hospitalized for the seventh time. I could just see the pain and disappointment on my husband's face. The agony and just hearing him say things like, "Why is this happening to me, I want to be the man I use to be, I want to provide for my family again because you should not have to do the things I am supposed to be doing, this should not be happening to me at the age of 54, a flu shot for 20 years in the Army and nothing happened why now?" He would say, "one shot almost took me away from my wife and children." Actually, it took me away because, we cannot do the things that we used to do, I cannot do the things that I used to be able to do with them or by myself. I can't go fishing, I can't go hunting, I can't go for a drive alone, I can't walk outside by myself, I can't do anything I used to do. Will I ever get better?"

Even while listening to my husband says those words, I hold on to this scripture-

Ephesians 3:16 He would grant you according to the riches of his glory to be strengthened with might by his spirit in the inner man.

CHAPTER 13

AM I DREAMING? I HAVE TO WAKE UP!

Is this a dream? Why am I in this hospital bed? I must be dreaming, I have to wake up; I have to take care of my husband. Oh no, this is real, I am in the hospital, I have had a heart-attack, the first of the two that I will have. It was December 2014, right before Christmas, I was home in Alabama with my family, visiting my mom and dad for the holidays. We had been there for my husband's father's funeral. My daughter took me to the community hospital because of the symptoms that I was having, where I then had to be rushed to the hospital in Pensacola, Florida. After being admitted to the hospital, I looked above my head, and hanging there was a large bottle of nitro-glycerin. Oh no, this could not be happening. I was in ICU. I was released on Christmas day. The second heart-attack was December of 2015; I was in the hospital for four days. Being a care-giver is not easy, because a lot of times you neglect taking care of yourself and don't realize what is going on with your own body. I had to re-group; I had to take better care of myself, so that I could take care of my family. I am still not at my best, but at least things are under control.

Jeremiah 17:14 - Heal me, o lord, and I shall be healed, save me and I shall be saved, for you are the one I praise.

CHAPTER 14

IN SICKNESS AND IN HEALTH

When the pastor gives the words for us to repeat, in sickness and in health, the first word is not one that we think about occurring within the first 35 years in a marriage, we think maybe after 50 or more years, at the age of 70 or older, but not before 30 years of marriage or even before the age of 55, but now as I think about those vows, you better believe that they take on an entire new meaning. I have been my husband's caregiver for the last five years. The stress of being a caregiver is awful and it can easily creep up on you. We try to mask it on the outside, but the inside is torn and beat down. I keep busy, but in moderation. I think I keep busy, because if I just sit, I know that I will start thinking about life before this, and become sad and overwhelmed and emotionally drained, so I just keep going. I continued to receive the strength to keep going. He knows that it is my desire to take care of my husband myself; I refuse to put him in a nursing home. I had to learn how to change out the colostomy bag and keep it clean. I had to learn to clean and pack my husband's bed sore, and make sure the wound vac was put on correctly at home. I had to learn to feed Melvin through a feeding tube, and flush it so that it would not get clogged up. I had to learn to give Melvin shots in his stomach so that he would not get blood clots, because he was unable to move around by himself.

Two years later the colostomy was removed and I had to pack the opening twice every day.

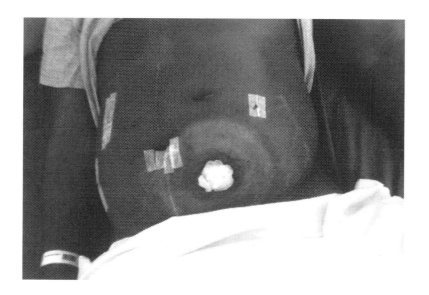

As long as I have been blessed and have my children and my strength, we will take care of Melvin. I do not want anyone else taking care of my husband. I love him and I want him to get well. Melvin is still very sick. There is nothing that can be done. The doctors have told me that there is no pill that will cure this illness. My husband can hardly eat or talk due to the paralysis in his throat.

Melvin is always depressed because he can't be the man he wants to be and the man that he used to be. He is a soldier; he will always be a soldier. He is a country boy; he grew up fishing, hunting, and enjoying the outdoors. He used to go out for drives, but now we have vehicles that he cannot even drive.

My husband is a provider, but he will never be able to work to provide for his family again. I long so much for my husband to recover, I pray for the day when we go on one of his doctor's visits, and they say that we have great news Donna, we have a cure for what your husband has, and after six months of treatment, he will be the man that you married and the father that your children knew. For now, Melvin will always need help with his everyday living because of his severe nerve damage.

I was looking forward to our retirement, when the two of us could sit down and relax, and just enjoy each other, or maybe we could just take a long overdue vacation if we so desire, but with my husband's illness, there may be a chance that we will not ever get to do it. Also, I look forward to seeing my husband get up in the wee hours of the morning, gathering his fishing equipment to catch fish for his family to eat. I look forward when the two of us could go to the restaurants or to a movie. I look forward to seeing my husband walking our daughter down the aisle at her wedding. I look forward to seeing my husband out in the yard making it beautiful like he had always done in the past. I look forward to seeing my husband playing and enjoying our grandkids one day, but most of all I look forward to just growing old with my husband.

I am believing and trusting for the best and keeping the faith; on June 22, 2016, Melvin had an appointment to see his throat doctor, the doctor told Melvin there was fluid and spots on his lung, so Melvin was given medication hoping that it would dry up the fluid. In my mind, I am saying oh no, here we go again, but I had to remember, that our steadfast faith has kept us this far and we will continue to trust in him and keep our faith.

On July 23, 2016, Melvin had to redo his x-ray, and was told he still had fluid on his lung, now the doctor has to draw the fluid off his lung and test it to make sure there is no cancer. I am now praying that everything is clear, because Melvin has been through too much, and I don't want him to get depressed again, something like that will be devastating to him, me and the children. Melvin is not a smoker, and has never been, so I am praying that it is not cancer. As I prayed, "Thank you God, it is not cancer". We will continue to trust and keep the faith in all things and to those of you reading this book, please continue to keep Melvin in your prayers.

A DREAM

(A Poem Written by My Daddy Mr. Theodore White)

I had a dream what heaven look like.

There was silver and gold that shined so bright. It all appeared to me one night.

There was Moses, John and Ezekiel, too.

They all made me welcome and said we are glad to see you.

They said we had trials and tribulation when we was living below But we don't have to worry about that any more.

Up here is love and joy and there is no hate. But to get here you must be straight.

And I looked around and there was Gabriel in his long bright robe. Out there not too far stood an old man Job.

He said I lost my family and all my friends, but I wouldn't let nothing stop me from making it in.

Up here is no sickness, death, or aches and pains. Every day with Jesus is the same.

My Daddy, Deacon Theodore White

I asked my children to share their thoughts and what they were feeling as they saw the suffering of their dad this is what my son Melvin Jr. shared:

LIFE INTERRUPTED

My thoughts on the events that took place during the time my dad fell ill were very stressful. It didn't help the fact I had just recovered from a mental melt-down not so long ago, during my years in Virginia. It was there that I learned the dread-ful news about my dad. I had finally found a new outlook on life, a new love in my life, and a new goal. However, that all had to be set aside for something more important, which was making sure that my family had help. Seeing that I was the only one that could even help didn't make the matters any better, in the end it seemed like I had to be what my dad was, which was the head of the house. Despite not making most of the more important decisions, I did get a job and started supporting my family little by little as I could, while balancing my aspirations. Day after day, I had to endure going to work with the stress of worrying about: if my dad would improve or grow worse, the health of my mother who was under the most stress, and my sister being able to have money to get to and from college. My health started to change as well as being diagnosed with acid reflux and bearing the pain that comes along with it. Mental stress and things on my mind began to break me down physically in my body, to the point it would hurt just to think of the next day. The only thing that gave me hope and perseverance, was that I realized that I was being strengthened, and I could withstand this awesome task that had come upon me. I needed to keep strong because my family was counting on me. One thing that I realized that this has prepared me, and has allowed me to understand and be ready to take care of and know my responsibilities as a husband and a father, if I were to get married one day. I spent my days working and studying to try and improve myself to try and find a better way to make things easier on me, so I could live a more productive life during hard times. At that point, acting on willpower was the only thing I could do to keep myself going. I had to endure the pain, the deep rooted anger I had for everyone that would not help, and most of all the people who caused this. As each month went by, my finances fluctuated as I tried to keep my family, my debts and my aspirations balanced in order to rebuild the life I lost, due to a mistake I made years prior to returning home. The stress began to change my way of thinking, I used to be passive, but lately, I have been becoming more aggressive because I knew that I was the only one that could protect them. Eventually, I came to a consensus that I have to be the one to bear the sins for them if they should come into any danger. I went from a son to a guardian; day and night I would be vigilant. Even as I sat at the computer many days, I kept my mind open to the world in order to know what is out there to shield my family from, and also be aware of what was around us at the time. One night, I heard someone trying to open our door, I think that night I scared myself, I never thought I would be in this situation. After that night, I sat back and wondered what happened to the old me. I guess in the end, this ordeal made me choose, do I want to sit back and let life and people take everything I love or do I stand up and fight back in order to hold on to everything I love in this world? I don't fear anyone anymore, only thing I fear is losing the heaven I got back after being alone for so long years ago. Even today, I still think of myself as their guardian and protector if danger or misfortune were to come to their door. I'm just blessed that I had the strength to help bring them back from the brink of disaster.

Melvin Jr

My Best Friend

Growing up with you was the best ever

I enjoyed playing basketball, fishing, and getting ran over by you on the softball fields

Also going bowling and falling over into a spiky bush because of you I'm glad I can call you my best friend

A few years passed, and I never thought I would come close to losing you for forever

You ended up in the hospital due to a flu shot and was in critical condition I just knew it was the end for me and you

As I saw you lying in the bed, I just couldn't comprehend why my best friend was slowly coming to an end

My best friend made it through the toughest 5 years of his life Now he's back home with his family safe and sound

I don't have my best friend completely back, but I'm glad he's still with us heading in the right path

The worst part about this whole journey is almost losing him from a stupid flu shot that's supposed to help people

In the end I'm glad I still have you here best friend You're the best dad and I love you

Your Baby Girl Shermiah

Shermiah

Mrs. Lula Thames Story

It all happened after my husband, Howard took the flu shot, my Howard was a great man, hardworking man, and he was one who never took off from his job. He would have vacation days and would not take the time off. For him to take off from his job, there was definitely something serious going on. He was a machine fixer at the carpet plant. He was 66 years old, and we had been married for 47 years, and he had been working at the plant for the last 47 years. He was a military veteran, who also served in the Army during the Vietnam War. On Wednesday, he told me that he would be taking the flu shot at work the next day. He said that the vaccine was being brought to the job. I told him, "okay." I had taken it once, and had become so ill that I vowed that I would never take it again, but nonetheless I didn't discourage him not to, for after all he was a healthy man, nothing to be worried about, so I thought.

Thursday came and Howard went to work, and he took the shot. He got home, went outside under the carport and began to read the newspaper, which he would purchase every day. This was his routine. I went outside and noticed that he was shaking something terrible. I asked him what was wrong. He said I don't know. I took the flu shot today. He began to feel worse. He told me that he was going to see his doctor tomorrow afternoon. Friday came and he went to see his doctor, but his doctor wasn't in, so he saw a female doctor who was working that day instead. She told him to take Mucinex, which he did.

Saturday morning came, he was still complaining that he wasn't feeling well, he was moping around the house, and he also complained of chest pains. He said maybe it will pass soon. He was trying to wait it out, hoping that it would go away. He told me that some of the other workers had taken the shot and were complaining of feeling funny, but I guessed that they must not have felt as bad as he did.

Sunday morning came, and I told Howard that I was going

50

to the store and that I would be back in a little while. He told me that he was still not feeling well, but he was going to get the carport swept. He loved keeping busy. He told me to go ahead. He said that if he continued to feel bad that he was going back to the doctor Monday.

When I arrived back home, Howard told me that while he was sweeping the carport he lost his breath. He came in and sat down. I asked him if he wanted to eat something. He told me that he did not have an appetite. I told him that I was going to eat me a little something. Later on, I told him that I was going to bed because I was tired.

I was awakened about ten minutes after I had fallen asleep, He came in looking awfully worried and told me that he felt something like a flame burning in his chest and that he could not breathe. He said call the paramedics. The paramedics came, he told them that he needed oxygen, because he couldn't breathe. They went back out and brought in the oxygen. They put everything on him and strapped him on the gurney. They took him to the hospital, I rode along, I was so worried, I was praying to the Lord. After they got him to the hospital, I went and sat in the waiting area. A few minutes had passed, I saw the doctor coming, and I knew that something wasn't right, something had gone wrong. Oh Lord, they told me that my Howard had passed away. I will never forget that day, October 25, when he took his last breath and died at Community Hospital in Atmore, Alabama.

It is not a day that goes by that I don't think of him. I have memories all around that I see of him every day. I said that it was nobody but the Lord who gave me strength to endure what I went through. I miss him so much, we were always together, doing things together. We were always there for each other. We talked about death, because we knew that one day that one of us would more than likely pass before the other. We would say that we are going to leave here one day, because as sure as we came here, we have to leave. I sure wasn't expecting this to happen, especially from the flu shot, because my husband was a healthy man.

It is something about 5:00 am, I have been getting up with Howard for all of those years he was getting up and going to work; we would eat breakfast and drink coffee together. I still get up, because I cannot lie in the bed, I get up and start my morning routine. Howard would leave the house around 6:20 am because the plant is not far from us, he didn't have that far to drive.

The other day I went upstairs and saw his computer and just sighed and said that he won't be coming back. I will find myself looking for him shortly after 3pm and I will say, he's not coming home, he is gone. I say to myself my Lord, I wasn't expecting him to go so quickly.

I live by the 23rd Psalm, and I was sharing with my sister one day and telling her that you have to meditate and live by it daily. I said without the Lord I know that I would not have made it. "God is my all and all."

Mrs. Ozzie Owens' Testimony

I took the flu shot in 2008. It was in Montgomery at the mall, the same year that the mall closed. My husband I stood waiting, I was in one line and he was in the other because the lines were extremely long. I took my shot, my husband took his shot, and again we were in two separate lines. One week later I began to feel weak and I started losing weight, I mean the weight was coming off, I wasn't doing anything to lose weight so that was very strange to me and why was I having this weakness. It got worse day by day. I had no appetite. My strength weakened. I couldn't even pull myself up. Oh my, what is going on? I knew something just wasn't right, something is wrong. I began to get worried, I prayed, I needed to know why I was feeling like this. I couldn't even get up the strength to stand straight. Lord, help me. I know that God watches over us and I look to him for everything. I even had to balance myself against the wall just to stand up. My husband was fine, he was going on with his everyday routine and activities, but I was feeling terrible.

I went to the doctor, the doctor didn't know what was going on. I got meds, they didn't work. I just called on Doctor Jesus. He is the greatest physician, I just prayed and prayed hoping to feel better.

One day I couldn't even get up, I was feeling terrible. I was in the room where a telephone was, Praises! I called my husband, he came home from work, and my husband did not like what he saw, the condition that I was in. He left and went to the doctor's office and told them that the meds that I had been given were not working and I was becoming more ill. My husband wasn't nice about it either. He is a God-fearing man, but he knew that he had to be firm and convince the doctor that this was serious and that his virtuous woman (because the scripture says in Proverbs 31, who can find a virtuous woman? For her price is above rubies, the heart of her husband doth safely trust in her, so that he shall have no need of spoil.

She will do him good and not evil all the days of her life) was not doing well at all. He wanted me to be taken care of and he was not playing around with my well-being. He wanted something to be done and be done immediately.

The doctor told my husband to go home and get me and bring me in and that a room would be waiting for me when he returned with me.

When I arrived at the hospital, they put me in a room. The nurse was trying to get my blood, but I have what they call rolling veins, so they had to put a port in. I was still suffering and suffering awfully bad. One night I heard the doctors discussing that they had never heard of or had seen what I was going through, but then the name Guillain-Barre' came up and they said that it comes from the flu shot. The female medical professional had controversy over whether to allow me to have the treatment, they went back and forth, and I mean it was a heated conversation. They were going back and forth. I guess that thought that I was asleep. All I could do was just pray to my God and ask him to intervene and just let me get the help that I needed. She told them something about there are 200 different viruses and she mentioned something about globulin but she was very very reluctant to allow me to be a candidate for the treatment. Other things were discussed, I heard something about the equipment was expensive for some treatment, the transportation from her office to the hospital would be costly, she went on and on about the cost of the treatment. These medical professionals went on with this for a couple of days. One evening one of the doctors came in after a meeting that they had. The doctor was upset and he said it has been a week and still no resolve. He said a lawsuit will come from this surely. Well, finally, they had an agreement about the compensation for the use of the equipment, treatment, etc.

The next night, around 10pm I was awakened and I was told that the treatment is going to begin. The treatment had to be extremely cold, frozen like, I could just think maybe like a frozen icee or slushee is what we used to called them a long time ago, you see I am 70 years old now.

They came in with a bag, hallelujah, God is good, and He is moving on my behalf, I serve a good God. They had to put it (the treatment) in through the port. Early the next morning, she asked me how I was feeling. I was feeling better just knowing that I was getting the treatment. The cost of the treatment was $4000.00 each time I got it. I had to get a lot of them. A nurse was sent home with me, he would sit until the meds finished going in through the IV. If I had to use the bathroom, he would unhook everything and when I would finish and return, he hooked me back up. He would sit and watch television, read, or talk to me until I was finished. This took anywhere from 2-3 hours. It was a slow drip, so it took some time. He did this every day for almost two weeks. I had home care, they had to come in and check on me.

I do want to share also that the nurses after seeing what happened to me and what I was going through they were refusing to take the shot. They got threatened that they would be terminated if they refused to comply. One of the staff feared that she would actually lose her job, she went ahead and took it and almost died. I felt so bad for her. I knew that it was a hard choice for her to choose because she didn't want to take the risk but also she needed her job to survive financially. I also had to do physical therapy to help with regaining my strength and movement in my body. The physical therapy would take two hours. They came out over a month, until I regained my strength. I had to have all kinds of equipment to help me due to my limited mobility, especially my bathroom, it had to be one that I could walk into easily without the danger of injuring myself. My husband and I joined a gym (specialized for my needs and folks that need it for cardiovascular) so that I could continue to have the right equipment that I needed to ensure that my muscles and joints stay strong.

Well, I am still here, although they told me that the illness can return. I keep my faith and trust in God. I know that he allowed me to get through it for a reason and that he left me here for a reason, many reasons, I can say. During the time of my illness and even now I say my favorite scriptures which are the 23rd Psalm

{A Psalm of David.}

The LORD is my shepherd; I shall not want.

He maketh me to lie down in green pastures: he leadeth me beside the still waters.

He restoreth my soul: he leadeth me in the paths of righteousness for his name's sake.

Yea, though I walk through the valley of the shadow of death, I will fear no evil: for thou art with me; thy rod and thy staff they comfort me.

Thou preparest a table before me in the presence of mine enemies: thou anointest my head with oil; my cup runneth over. Surely goodness and mercy shall follow me all the days of my life: and I will dwell in the house of the LORD forever. and Matthew 5:8-Blessed are the pure in heart, for they will see God.

I know that I will tell Him thank and allowing me to keep a pure and clean heart in spite of what I went through.

THANKS TO THE MEDICAL STAFF

To the doctors, nurses, aids, medical clerks, housekeeping, dining facility workers, lab and x-ray technicians, and hospital volunteers. Thank you.

VERY SPECIAL THANKS TO DOCTOR MEGBEW OKOROBA

To Doctor Megbewe Okoroba,

Words can't express the sincere thanks and gratitude my family and I have for you and your amazing staff. Your professionalism shows in your work with the love and kindness you put into caring for my husband.

It is a true blessing that you came into my husband's life as his physician and our children and I am glad that you were sent by a divine intervention and you were making sure Melvin received and continues to get the help he needs to survive his illness and most of all just being there when he need you most.

I would recommend Doctor OKOROBA to the world because he is one of the best caring Physician you will find and he always takes pride in making sure all of his patients get the care they need.

Also I would like to thank his Neurologist, Gastrologist, Hospitals, etc. and their entire staff for a job well done. I pray blessings from God to each of you for the care that you continue to give to my husband Melvin.

THANK YOU TO MY FAMILY

Thanks to my brother Anthony White and his wife Verlynn of Pensacola, Florida, for taking time from their busy schedules in making sure our mother, Mrs. Louise White, arrived to our home safely to take care of our daughter, Shermiah, while I was with my husband during his hospital stay in Atlanta.

Thanks to my sister Paula White in Huntsville, Al. for her love and support during our time of need.

Thanks to my brother Theodore White, Jr. of Atmore, Al., for his love and support.

PASTOR JOHN SAMUEL (THE ANGEL)

Thank you to Pastor John Samuel for contacting me around 2:00pm one Saturday afternoon, alerting me that you had gone by to see my husband and he was sleeping so you did not wake him. I said to myself that it wasn't like my husband to not wake up when someone came to visit. I called the hospital and the nursing staff informed me that he hadn't been responsive since 4am. I hurried to the hospital, very upset and worried. My heart was crushed and must have dropped to my stomach when I entered into the room and saw my husband lying there only with a diaper on, he looked lifeless and helpless. How can this be? what happened?, I cried out. I was told that he had a seizure and that he had slipped into a coma. Oh my poor Melvin, I was so hurt, but I prayed for God's strength to help me through this journey.

BAKERY FRIENDS

Melvin worked with the most wonderful group of people, they went far and beyond their duties to help my family during my husband Melvin's time of illness. Their acts of kindness will always be remembered and never forgotten, without them we would not have made it. Our friends at the bakery made sure that we had food to eat, gas for the car to get back and forth to the hospital, and most of all to pay our bills for the month. For that, we love them, it was never easy for me to ask for help because of my pride; we will always love and think of our bakery friends as family forever, I pray may God forever bless you all.

THANKS TO MY BEST FRIEND

Yolanda Wilson, thank you for everything you have done to help make this book a success. Without your hard work and your dedication, this would not have been possible. From the first time we met at a local beauty salon 20 years ago in Missouri, I knew I had found a dear friend, one that would be there forever. After three years at Fort Leonard Wood in Missouri, our husbands PCSed to different locations, and three years later Divine Intervention put two friends back together. I thank him so much, because friends like you are very hard to find. You are a rare gift. You are a treasure to my family, and I know only a friend like you could have known what we needed. I will forever be thankful to you, and I can't thank you enough.

Printed in the United States
By Bookmasters